A Boutique Bouquet of Poems and Stories

By Elliot M. Rubin

Copyright November 2017
Library of Congress

ISBN 978-0-9981796-1-2
ISBN 0-9981796-1-2

Dedication

To my wife, Laura,
for her incredible grace and kindness,
and for the fifty years, she rode the crests
and wipeouts of married life with me.

In Memory of

Herman S. Rubin
Who wrote poetry and
short stories all his life

Preface

These poems and stories are written for your
enjoyment. While most of them are based on reality,
many of them are my personal experiences and feelings
. Some may be open to discussion, some are
humorous, but most importantly they are in plain
English
You do not need an advanced degree in literature to
appreciate these poems and stories.
Please enjoy them.

Other books by the author are:

Hot Cash Cold Bodies [first in a series]
Khara Bennet - Vengeance [second in the series]
Khara Bennet - Dead Girls Don't Die [third in the
series]
Romance and Murder in Bensonhurst
Scrambled Poems from my Heart
The Phartick Chronicles

www.CreativeFiction.net

Table of Contents

Guys on the Corner

They sit on the stoops
from noon till night,
watching traffic
stop and go,
commenting…
on sports teams
they like,
not doing much
but
talking bout stuff.

Their future is
bleak,
not exciting,
joking around,
skipping school,
too often
not realizing
they will fail
to succeed,
wasting their time
hanging
on the street.

Cool stuff they want
but can't afford,
excited to see lifestyles
they'll never attain,
laid back smoking something,
not trying to work,
they let their whole life
pass them by with part-time
dead end jobs,
in a dead-end life.

Holidays in Manhattan

an Arctic front roars in from the north,
the wind is blowing everything about,
snowflakes swiftly fall and cover the ground,
its holiday magic seems so pure and holy.

downtown train grates are covered with men,
trying to warm them from the bitter cold,
tattered and ragged with ill-fitting clothes,
soiled and unwashed with lice on their skin,
feeding themselves from a large dumpster bin.

while uptown folks sing as they skate on rink ice,
buying gifts to present to family and friends.
and leaving their meal half-eaten and wasted,
with no thought of feeding those without food.

a holiday of good cheer, and all of that stuff,
we gather around with those that we love,
forgetting the ones without any hope,
sleeping on streets with nowhere to go.

no one alone can solve these big problems,
what do we do for the poor souls without?
we are warmed by the hearth, and the love of dear ones,
yet many tend to stand motionless, frozen in place,
doing nothing.

In a Corner

At dusk one day as I walked home from work,
  I passed a side door in the dark, dank alley
Of a large, faded, old red-brick building
  Built in the booming fifties after the war.
The cries of a young child caught my attention,
  Set back in the dark corner of a little-used entrance,
I saw curled up a seven-year-old sobbing,
  Into unwashed cupped hands held to its face,
And tears cascading down its arms.
  With delicate features, and a beautiful, gentle face,
 I could not tell if it was a boy or a girl.
  Close-cropped brown hair matted and oily,
Unwashed clothes, stains, and soil easy to see.
  I hesitated to approach; afraid of being involved.
Yet the cries of a child echoed against the walls
  Crashing head-on into my heart; I asked if I could
Help, why are you crying?
  I am hungry, and only had a piece of bread since
yesterday.
In a country of great wealth, I found a child
  Living a third world existence, bathe in poverty,
And only a short bus ride away,
  From the wealth, and elegance, of snooty Park
Avenue.
I opened the takeout bag I bought for dinner,
  Set it out with a plastic knife, fork, and napkin,
Then sat on the concrete watching my food be
devoured,
  While I curled up and sobbed into my washed cupped
hands.

Questions

Why does the color of a person's skin matter?
  Black, white, red, and yellow,
And the infinite shades God created in-between.

If every person is related inside,
  And our organs are now interchangeable.
We are all brothers and sisters;
  Isn't it time we acted like it?

Why did a husband decline a lifesaving operation
  Which he really needed, but is afraid
If he dies, his widow will be left penniless?

Why do we send billions each year to the
  Swiss bank accounts of third world strongmen,
Instead of cradle to grave care of our own?

Why is a convicted racist pardoned?
  Because he did his job profiling,
And detaining people of color?

Justice Justice, you shall pursue…
  Is it more than only a bible phrase?
I believe it is an ethical way of life for all.

What happened to kindness and caring,
  And basic human decency for each other?
Finally, where is the love…where is the love?

Regrets about Barbara

Sitting by the telephone
  Waiting for it to ring,
Her mind must wander aimlessly,
  Why didn't he call back?

We went to high school together,
  And flirted back and forth,
I liked her bouncy spirit,
  But I never asked her out.

My pal and I went out one night,
  And drove to Wolfies to grab a bite,
She was at the counter with a friend,
  But something about her had changed.

She went from good to amazingly cute,
  Her curly hair was now long gone,
The cut she had intrigued me,
  I waved and walked right over.

We started to date, I liked her,
  But her twin brother glared at me,
So I never went too far with her,
  Though I enjoyed her company.

She asked me to a costume party,
  Her sorority had in Manhattan,
Going on the subway in costume
  Wasn't my style at all.
Too immature to tell her,
  I never called her back.

The Picture

Every day my heart and soul craves for you,
  When the sun rises in the east and sets in the west.

My mind is in chaos, and my thoughts rumble
  Through my brain, thinking only of you.

Holding you close was a sweet dream come true,
  My love is so real I can feel it right now.

Time marches on, and our youth is long gone,
  Your memory lives in me as real as today,

We had something special I will never forget,
  I read of your death below your picture;
    my sadness is overflowing.

True Love

Too many people fall in love
Without really knowing
Who they are themselves.

How can you really know a person
That you want to spend the rest
Of your life with,
When you are not sure
What kind of human being
You really are?

Don't
Rush to Love.
It will come naturally
If at all.
Then it is a
True Love.

Half

The picture is torn in half.

Only I am shown sitting in my bedroom, on my bed, at my parent's summer house at Lake Hopatcong. The black and yellow vertical stripes I painted on the wall only show in black and white. The girl I was dating the year before I met my wife is missing from the other side of the photograph.

I forgot all about it until my parents sold their home, moved from Brooklyn to New Jersey, and cleaned out my old room. "Who tore this?" I asked. My father answered he did, "why?"

How could I tell him I wanted a keepsake of this seventeen-year-old girl? She was in the grand finales of the Miss Teenage America contest, was cute as a button, and had her picture in a national teen magazine as one of the finalists.

I never thought of myself as cool, confident maybe, but definitely not cool. With a full head of Fonzie like curly hair, a white jacket with the collar turned up, a skinny one hundred thirty pounds and five foot ten, my picture, when I look at it brings back memories of my teenage years.

Dating a different girl each week during the summers, swimming in the lake and speeding around on my old, used, 1939 Chris Craft brings good times back to life. It was a waterborne hot rod, beat up with holes in the side just above the waterline, and about to sink, but it was fast. If I stopped in the middle of the lake, the engine would never restart. So whomever I was with had to spend some quality time with me; it was too far to swim. The girls thought I did it on purpose. Maybe, but the engine would really never restart once it was heated; something to do with the coil. Eventually, when it cooled down I was able to bring my date back to shore where we would jump in the water; then go for something to eat at Bertrand's Island amusement park.

Maybe, looking back, in reality, I really was 1960's cool?

Aging

The older I become,
The more I begin to realize,
My future is in my past,
And the days ahead are numbered.

The risks I took in my youth,
Without any fear or trepidation,
Knowing there is always tomorrow,
And I can get back up again.

Now I look at things too deeply,
Not able to measure in my head,
The outcomes of my decisions,
As clearly as I once was able.

It was never money, power or prestige,
Which drove me to strive in life
Although they are nice to have and use,
But a desire and push to accomplish.

I saw the humor in many events,
And laughed at my heart's content,
The simple things are so much better,
As I hold my grandchild in my arms.

This is what is essential,
A no holds barred real love,
Without the frills of society
Playing havoc with our emotions.

Just love with all your heart,
And wake up every morning.
Placing your feet firmly on the ground,
While taking a long deep breath of air.

You've notched another day of life,
Be cheerful with all you meet,
Too soon you'll be a memory,
To those who loved you back.

Bessie Trauner Greenberg

The Angel of Death is standing, with frustration, in the doorway.

My parents are standing with my aunts and uncles gathered around each side of my grandmother Bessie's bed…waiting. I am sixteen and remember the white blanket covering her frail body so she would be warm. She was a short woman, made of steel, who as a young immigrant girl married my grandfather due to a promise to her mother, and not out of love for him. On her mother's deathbed, she promised, at fifteen, to take care of her three younger siblings. After her death, a distant aunt took in my grandmother, and her two sisters, but did not want Bessie's young brother, so he was placed in an orphanage.

A man in America said he would marry my grandmother if she came to New York. He paid for the passage over from Austria and committed to bringing her siblings too after the marriage. With determination, she traveled alone to a strange new country. But he backed out of his promise, said he would not bring them over, and she did not marry him once she was in New York.

On the rebound, my grandfather, a friend of her ex-fiancé stepped in and said he would bring them over if she would marry him. He kept his word, her younger siblings were reunited with her and lived with them until they grew up and moved out. My grandfather was not an educated man, and not the ideal husband. When he went on a vacation in the hot and humid New York City summers, he never took her with him. She was left with her three children and siblings for a week or two while he was in the cool mountains. He was rough around the edges, a hard-working Romanian while my grandmother was homeschooled, and educated by tutors in Austria as a young girl.

Many years later her heart wore out, and the minutes are fleeting for a final goodbye.

I was ushered in to see her for one last time at her request. "Give me a kiss," she asked. I leaned over, and gently kissed her cheek. Looking at me with open eyes she raised her hand to place it around my neck pulling me closer to her face; a kiss on my lips I will never forget. Then she closed her eyes, and I was ushered out of the room hearing the cries of mourning in the background. One Angel took another.

When I went to kindergarten and first grade, she would cross a busy avenue to pick me up for lunch every day in the afternoon. To encourage me to eat she would tell me about Moishe Kapoya, a Yiddish story about a boy who did things backward. This she did while smoking unfiltered Camel cigarettes, drinking Maxwell House coffee black, and listening to As the World Turns on the radio. A true multi-tasker before the term existed.

Yes, of the seven grandchildren I was her favorite. Because I was her only daughter's son I stood out from my male cousins. Her two sons, my uncles, had wives, and they only visited every so often. But my mother brought me to her home every day. There is a special bond between a mother and daughter. My grandmother proved this point during her lifetime.

Although she now resides in infinity, my grandmother lives on every day in my mind's eye.

Unrequited Love

I am unsure of your reaction,
  If I told you that I love you.
Will you return my true affection?
  Or break my heart into small pieces?

I watched you from afar,
  We spoke a little once,
I don't think we'll ever join,
  I feel alone, and insecure.

We met in private places,
  A friend's home some weeks ago,
Our paths too often pass,
  It seems we always smile.

At night I plan the future,
  A picket fence around our home,
But I am so much older,
  My heart is filled with doubt.

You're alive and feeling vibrant,
  Jumping through life's events with youthful zest,
While I cherish a good night's sleep,
  And pray I wake tomorrow.

If I was a little bit younger,
  And you a bit more aged,
Our story might be written,
  They lived happily ever after.

Love Is...

Love is
eating a cold
sweet
watermelon
on a hot day;
hugging someone
who hugs you back;
A baby smiling
at you for the first time;
when a lover says yes to you,
someone kissing you first,
giving of yourself
to someone else,
holding hands
for the first time,
and holding someone
tight in your arms,
cuddling
with a special person,
thinking
of their feelings first,
and not asking why?
Love is acceptance.
Love is hard to find.

Magic

The summer days float by so slow,
And lazy ways come to the front.
Young boys and girls sprint around,
Their hormones raging uncontrolled.

Since a magnet has two sides,
Opposites do attract,
The lovers meet and kiss again,
With a strong embrace, they hug at last.

Maybe it is chemistry,
Others say its nature.
Believers swear it is foretold,
But I believe it is pure magic.

Reflecting

The road I walked is a long one,
  Compared to some friends who are gone
With twists and turns too numerous,
  Yet we all end up together.

The mountains in life are high,
  And most often hard to climb,
The rewards are usually commensurate,
  With the effort, and sometimes not.

Of course, there are valleys,
  And often we see them first,
Causing us to stop and question,
  Should we go forward on our quest?

The smile on my face is constant,
  Due to family and friends I have.
Happiness is to be shared,
  Not sealed away and misered.

Love is not a Hippie byword,
  To be used with little passion,
But meant to bring you in,
  To a warm and inviting heart.

Inner Peace

How far do you have to travel to find inner peace?

Some people travel through their whole lives and never find it. Yet it's right there for them if they stop, and think about it.

Often we read about famous people who have climbed to the mountain tops on their path of life, yet they have challenges and turmoil running rampant in their lives. The truth is every mountain has a valley, and we have to realize how we can negotiate those valleys to find that inner peace.

There is a common denominator that twelve-step programs use called a higher power. For many people, this is their life rope to getting in a good place mentally and in life.

In some ways, people are like salmon. They are born in a stream then swim out to the oceans, and live their lives; sometimes far away from where they started.

But just like salmon people know where they came from. They may not admit to it or acknowledge it, but it is there in the inner space of their being.

And sometimes they manage to swim back to the place of inner peace just by sitting in a sanctuary. They don't have to read or say anything. Just to be seated, and surrounded by the holiness of a place where they can feel a higher power, and often they will find that warm and comforting inner peace.

Humility

It takes guts
to say you are
sorry,
Not everyone can
do it.

In retrospect,
when I think
of all the
girls
I have loved,
I want to take
this time
to say

I
am
sorry…

for setting
the bar
so high
in your life.

The Last Hug

Years ago
a picture in the
New York Daily News
is seared into my memory.
A father is kneeling on a beach
holding his young dead son.
The tide is lapping
at his feet
while he held the lifeless small body
in his arms,
pressed against his chest;
his head bent forward
in grief.

The boy unfortunately
drowned.
There was no story
to the picture,
only the headline over it.
The grief the father must have felt
is unimaginable to me.

I can only conceptualize
his feelings and wish no one else
ever feels his pain.

But there is a lesson
from seeing this picture.
We have to hug
the ones we love as if it is the last hug.

Life is too short, too fast,
and we cannot get back the time we lost.

Don't say I'm sorry,
say I want a hug.
Say I love you.
You might not get another chance.

Belief

The wind can blow and fell a tree,
   It swoops down and removes my hat,
My face turns red from a gusty chill,
   I can't see it, but I know it's there.

When I look into my grandchild's face,
   My heart beats a little faster,
Without touching it, my body feels
   Love exists, yet I cannot see it.

There are some things we feel,
   There some things we do not see,
There are some things we do not understand,
   Yet we know they do exist.

The Door

Love is a strange thing to try and control.
Sometimes it occurs when you least expect it,
And stays for years and years, and sometimes not.
The length of time is immaterial,
Romance is but a life experience.
When your heart is breaking and hurt,
Remember you are not alone,
Others too have suffered.
This is not an uncommon thing.
Yet we continue our search
For the elusive everlasting amour.
Cupid shoots an arrow through a red heart,
Though it never bleeds it can hurt so deep.
The path of life is winding, and the future
Is unknown, as we continue to walk
The hallways of love, seeking out the
The door to happiness, and our one true love.

Caring

In kindergarten, poor Ray did not speak,
  And was sent to school without any food,
Or a coat in the middle of winter,
  While his siblings were well fed and dressed.

He lived on the other side of the tracks,
  With it's true to life terrible thoughts and deeds,
The teachers brought him milk and cereal,
  To eat alone in the nurse's office with her.

All week they chipped in for his food,
  And brought him lunch so he could eat,
Every day he had two meals at least,
  And dinner was a rare occasion.

He never had a bath or shower,
  The school nurse would wash him up
Alone behind her closed wood door,
  So other kids would not smell him in school.

After three he had to play outside,
  No matter how cold the weather had been,
He was not allowed inside till dark,
  While mom entertained new found "uncles."

The principal bought him shoes and socks,
  And a warm winter coat one year.
The next day he came to school,
  Wearing a sweater in the freezing cold.

Seems mom sold the coat for cash.
  The principal bought another,
Incensed she warned she'd call child services,
  If ever his coat is sold again.

They left him back every year in school,
  So they could protect from abuse at home,
And feed him, so he had some food,
  Until he grew up and left the system.

Humanity

The guest house of humanity
  Is either full or empty,
People showing kindness, or not,
  Smiles or frowns, it is never dull.
Sometimes… it is just life.

Recognition

My name has no meaning
  It does not stand for anything
Yet my soul cries out
  I am here, I am here

Cosmos

What is life about?
Love, good deeds,
Hate and evil?

When the sun
Turns red, and
Sucks in the planets
One billion
Years from now;
Everything we hold dear
And treasure
Will be lost
To the blackness
Of infinity

Hate will be
Vanquished

Love will be
Gone

Life will
Cease

Death will be
Permanent

Nothingness
Will rule
The universe

Dad's Death

They asked me if I wanted to look
one last time,

Before they sealed my father's coffin
shut forever?

I decided to remember him laughing
out loud,

And feeling his touch and warmth
on my skin.

If I close my eyes, I can always
see him.

Memories

     "I'm sorry," the surgeon said. "The steroids he is on for over twenty years, to control his kidney disease, caused his veins to become tissue paper thin. They were not able to hold a suture near his heart. He passed away during the operation due to an aneurysm."

     There is no waiting room near this wing of the hospital. My mother and I sat silently on a hard wooden bench in the hallway. We are trying to understand what he told us; Dad is gone. At three in the morning, the surgical unit is as silent as death.

     I realized the cocoon I lived in, knowing my father is there to help me in case I needed him for any reason, ceased to exist at that moment. Now I must spread my wings on my own. I alone had to decide which direction to fly knowing there is no longer a safety net of experience and knowledge behind me.

     Before the operation, we sat with him in a small room when the doctor asked us to walk into the hall for a moment. We are informed the pretesting the surgical group looked at told them my father had a ten percent chance of survival.

     Without hesitation, Mom and I agreed to go ahead and operate. Any chance, no matter how small, is better than doing nothing, and sure death.

     Mom kisses him goodbye before the nurses pushed the bed out the door. They are heading for the operating room as I walked alone alongside the bed holding his hand.

Everybody stopped at the pneumatic doors as they opened wide welcoming him to his fate. His legs are covered in mounds of heated blankets to keep them warm due to poor circulation as I looked at my father for the last time

Although I enjoyed a lifetime of bonding in business, and at home with my father, I felt there is something I needed to tell him I had not said before; "Dad, I love you."

"I know you do" was his reply. We never spoke again.

Father

I never knew my father as I was growing up.

He left early in the morning
to go meet his clients, and at night
go to the furniture store he owned with his
brother.
I ate my six Oreos with milk for breakfast
and went to school
not seeing him for days.

This went on my whole life while I was at
home.

We lived in the same house
but never really met.
Until his kidney disease kept him home,
and I took over the family business.
I rarely spoke with him;
except for business reasons
which were every day.

My father wrote poems, letters, and essays
his whole life
when he had the time to do so.
Often
he asked me to read his papers.
It was just stuff to me,
an old man's writings.
Not interested.

Then he passed away when I was in my forties.
Someday...
you'll appreciate what I write
Dad often said to me.

Cleaning out his files
I came upon those papers,
all handwritten.

After he died,
I first met my father.

My Mother's Voice

The kids are asleep, and my wife is upstairs,
  The late news is over, and the lights are turned down.
The silence is comforting as I think of my life,
  When in my ear my mother speaks softly to me.

The past just then roars back to my youth,
  Protected from harm and smothered with love.
Not a care in the world, and my future ahead,
  I smile, lay back, and welcome the past.

My mother is sitting and stroking my head,
  Grandma is ironing my sheets so I'm warm,
A cold wind is blowing and it's freezing outside,
  But I'm sleepy and cuddled and ready for bed.

Goodnight my love I'll see you tomorrow,
  I'll take you to school and bake you a treat,
I remember her voice as clear as a bell,
  My eyes swell up with tears streaming down.

Every time I hear my mother's sweet voice,
  My heart aches and hurts I miss her so much,
Into my ears, she whispers so often,
  It's as if she'll never leave me alone.

Piano Memories

Looking back it's like a Disney dream,
  My mother playing piano after lunch,
Before my sister and I return to school,
  Singing together while she plays songs for us.

The Davy Crockett songbook contained the tunes,
  The television show played on Sunday nights,
While my sister belted out a Cinderella song,
  Bibbidi-Bobbidi-Boo.

The baby grand was melodically beautiful,
  Needing a tune-up every now and then,
There was nothing to be done with our untrained voices,
  Except to play louder and soldier on.

It is sitting in Florida at my sister's lovely home,
  With a cracked soundboard aged like us,
This piano does more than just play music,
  It is a repository of memories from long ago.

A Lost Career Opportunity

It is a felony in New York, but I did it anyway.

My defense would have been I am only seventeen, and didn't know any better. The guys on the block and I used to play card games gambling with plastic chips. Then one-day lightning struck me. I decided to use the empty attic in my parent's home since it was never used.

Upstairs on the vacant third floor where nobody ever ventured are two small bedrooms with a full bath. So I decided why waste the empty space as I saw an opportunity to make money.

I hired two of my friends and opened a gambling casino.

The vision was to grow a little wealth while in high school. There was a roulette table, a 21 table, a mini improvised slot machine, and a toy electric horse racing game they could bet on.

The first two days went well, and the place was humming with activity. Based on her poor reputation, I "hired" the strawberry blond a grade ahead of me. She was my hostess and the "entertainment."

Then on the third day, the Feds walked upstairs in the guise of my mother. She was wondering why dozens of teenage boys she didn't know were traipsing through her home and going upstairs.

My career in Las Vegas was suddenly cut short. By default, others now had the opportunity to build billion dollar edifices in the desert.

Thanks, Mom.

Pressure in my Mind

The walls are closing in on me
  As the silence in my room
Is Deafening. The lights are off
  And my mind is wandering.

Everyone is gone
  Somewhere or other,
But I don't remember
  Where.

The sun has set and the
  Shades are up. Darkness
Permeates the room while
  I look out the window at nothing.

This is not normal I say to myself,
  As I continue to stare at the walls.
By myself with no one around
  The loneliness is crushing.

Stuff Called Life

As we run through our life
  We really never see,
The scenery flashing by,
  Is what life is all about

Slow down and start to walk,
  Through the gardens, we call
Our life, experiences we
  Encounter influences us each day.

The puppy love we remember,
  The one we know got away that day,
Our broken dreams of being together,
  Was never taken seriously by the other.

And the sobering thought of being alone,
  Remembering the touching of each other's hand,
Never fled from our minds when a new love
approached,
  The flames of passion are seared into our hearts.

We grew and matured as time came and went,
  The days grow shorter as our minds fly back,
To the times we ran with our hearts on our sleeve,
  No worries, our endless life lies just ahead.

The serenity of family as laughs fills the house,
  These are the things we should cherish and hold.
The little things we might miss as we too grow old,
  Should stop us to look, and remember them all.

Life is not long and in some way too short,
  Open yourselves up to grab it all in.
The good times and bad are the things we all have,
  We call it our life, so slow down a bit.

Look at the trees, and the friends we did make,
  Taste the goodness and savor it all.
The kindness and love you have in your heart,
  This is the stuff our life is being made of.

Nobody Said….

Nobody gave me a free ride,
Nobody told me anything at all,
Nobody gave me a choice to decide,
Nobody said that life is easy.

I had no choice when to be born,
I had no choice to pick a home,
I had no choice to choose my parents,
Nobody said that life is easy.

My DNA selected me from others,
My body and brain are programmed from it,
My processes function as well as can be,
Nobody said that life is easy.

I persevered and claimed success,
I have a heart and empathy too,
I try to help others as best I can,
Nobody said that life is easy.

At the end of the day, I sit and think,
At events, I encountered during my days,
At the good times and bad, my memory returns,
Nobody knows…I am exhausted from life.

Hearing

In my youth, I never heard the footsteps of God,
  Concentrating my energies on the future to come,
Work, play and supporting a family were goals,
  Plus new cars, clothes, and growing my business.

In middle age, I started to tire, slow down, broken body,
  Bones ached, muscles hurt, aches and pains were my
Companions for years. Then one day I stopped
  And listened; I began to hear the footsteps of God.

In my old age as I sit in retirement, and think back,
  The material things I valued had no worth,
Only relationships with people are of merit.
  Listening, now I hear God knocking on my door.

Rose

I remember the morning of my 70th birthday, at 8 a.m., while I was walking the circle around my block as I do every morning. For some reason, I started to think of Rose.

I don't remember her last name, but I know her story, and her face is as vivid in my memory as if I saw her yesterday.

It was only once I met her, and it was for a very short period time while she shopped in my old Brooklyn furniture store many years ago.

As she walked in at a snail's pace through the entry doors, I saw a petite, gaunt-looking, and white-haired less than five feet tall elderly Jewish woman. The store phone rang, and I asked my sales manager Laura to please assist her. When my phone call was finished, I walked back onto the sales floor and saw both of them talking in the rear of the store.

When Rose made her purchase and left I asked Laura what they were talking about. I was told that Rose, in a short period of time, communicated to her the current situation in life she is experiencing. Her late husband had a heart condition and needed a lifesaving surgery. But he refused to have it because he didn't want to spend all of their life savings on the operation; he had no health insurance. His concern was that if he didn't survive the surgery, she would be alone, penniless and broke. So he did not have the operation, his heart gave out, and he passed away.

Rose explained to Laura she is now alone in the world. She is an only child, has no cousins or other relatives, and her husband never wanted to have children. She enjoyed speaking to Laura undisturbed.

Today as I walked my daily route, and thought of Rose, I then thought of the birthday party my family is having for me that afternoon. My children and seven grandchildren will be there as will nieces and nephews.

Why I asked myself, do some people oppose helping those truly in need? What is so terrible about enabling all people to have health insurance? We literally give trillions of dollars away each year to foreign countries that squander the money and don't help their starving underdeveloped nation. Why can't we support our own citizens?

This phrase comes to mind "there but for the grace of God go I."

We should be mindful of it and count our blessings.

A Trip to Manhattan

Seeing the crowd move in Penn Station,
  Rushing below ground to get to their train,
Hustling before it leaves New York underground,
  I can feel cool air blowing in from above.

The noise of traffic filters down through the maze,
  With shrill muffled car horns trumpeting together,
And people talking while streaming to get home,
  Eyes focused on the sidewalk or on their cell phone.

Taxi, Taxi, the doorman calls out to the street,
  As a yellow cab pulls over and the doors fling open.
Hoping in we say Hunter College please, and the
cabdriver's
  Radio blasts a southern soul sermon.

Satan's mother-in-law is still alive he preached,
  She is watching out what you are doing.
I said to myself she must have sent this traffic,
  Slowly block by block the torture seems endless.

The taxi stops and lets us out, we walk
  A block or two before we enter,
I love to walk the streets of Manhattan,
  The electric vibes tingle through the crowds,
The best show on Broadway is free to all,
  Watching people is really great theater.

Then we pass through security with nearly a thought,
  And escalate up to the third-floor hall,
To listen to a writer speak to the group,
  About her thoughts on writing a book.

Her words meandered all over the place,
  Offering advice on why she wrote this,
I picked up a phrase to remember this day,
  About Satan's mother-in-law in a yellow city cab.

Pews to Brooklyn

I have been advertising online to sell the two front pews from the synagogue. A gentleman answered the ad and asked to visit and look at them. I almost didn't answer his call as it was a Las Vegas phone number and thought it is a crank robocall, but it wasn't.

He came, and I showed him the pews, then we started to talk.

The gentleman lived in Las Vegas before his divorce and came from Brooklyn, in fact, my old neighborhood. He resembled one of the television show's Sopranos bigger guys. I felt right at home listening to his accent with deese, dems and doe's. We knew each other's places and reminisced a little about the old days.

Being curious I asked if he needed them for a church. He smiled and said no.

"I belong to a smoking club in Brooklyn. We're about 25 to 30 guys."

At that moment I knew who I was talking with. He continued speaking.

"The club was sold to a Pakistani guy… and we just don't feel him. So we went looking for another place. I bought a bus and thought we could put these in there facing each other with a table between them. This way the wood is easier to clean and won't hold a smoke odor like upholstery would."

He left to go measure the interior of the bus and told me he will get back to me if interested.

Ah, the old Brooklyn guys I left behind are still roaming the streets.

A Loss

The goalie is a mountain of a man,
  Standing on ice skates in front of the net,
Fearlessly facing the oncoming tide
  With only a stick, a glove, and a mask.

They slam the puck with all their might,
  As it flies across the ice,
At one hundred miles an hour,
  He deflects it to the side.

Again the attackers advance for blood,
  Passing the rubber puck with speed,
While the goalie watches every move,
  And with cat-like reflexes, he responds.

A jumble of players mix it up,
  Only feet in front of him,
Gleaming skates twirl and slide so fast,
  While the passing puck is caught in limbo.

To the left, and then the right
  He shifts his massive frame.
The puck comes out of nowhere,
  To land behind his glove.

The bells go off, and sirens too,
  A score has just been made,
The goalie removes his heavy mask,
  And bows his head in grief.

The home team has lost the game.
  They missed the qualifying mark,
To enter the next month's finals,
  And go home in complete defeat.

Supermarket Poker

Standing in line, I am watching a lady
  Place her groceries on the market's counter.
The cashier slowly takes a piece,
  And swipes each one to total the order.

Ninety-five fifty she says to the woman.
  Opening her pocketbook, she took out her purse,
With two rows of credit cards stacked on each side,
  Deciding which card to play at the moment.

Does she throw out the one for the high airline miles?
  Or the red bank card for some small money back?
Playing the game…she picks the store card,
  And hands it over for an instant price cut.

Mystery

The thunder clouds roiled overhead,
  With buckets of water beating down,
Only the pings of the droplets,
  Resounded against the window glass.

The hotel was old and vintage,
  With few guests now in the rooms,
A single bulb glared from my bathroom,
  As I lay beneath my sheets.

Howling wind blew the tree leaves,
  Against the side of my darkroom,
The halls were dank and empty,
  No one dared to walk outside.

On the beat of twelve at midnight,
  A scream was heard by me,
I opened my door to peek outside,
  And saw a body lying there.

There is no blood or weapon, on the floor or in the hall,
  Yet here lays a deceased person, I never saw before.
The police came and inspected, they said it was a crime,
  There were no marks on the body, but they found a
clue no less.

This is not the first time; they found a case like this.
  Unknown is the assailant, who leaves a golden tooth.
So when you travel far and wide or stay the night
  Somewhere, look for a person smiling, and missing a
precious tooth.

Life as a squirrel

Ever wonder what it's like to be a squirrel?

Flying up the tallest of trees,
trying to escape from a chasing cat,
with four short legs moving very fast.

Waving your tail to balance your gait
 while holding on to an uneven tree.

The sounds of barking at the hungry cat,
chase it away before it climbs after you.

But stuck high up near the top of the tree,
the dog will chase you if you dare come down.

He won't eat you like the hungry cat,
to him, it's a game…and surprise you are it!

The Hunt

Buzz
I didn't get much sleep last night.

Buzz
All I heard was this sound in my ear.

Buzz
Turning on the lights, I hunted,

Buzz
My caveman is rushing forth,

Buzz
To smite the beast seeking my blood,

Buzz
With curled up paper I looked around,

Buzz
Until it landed on my lamp,

No more Buzz,
No more lamp,

Now more sleep?

The Mighty Can Fall

He was not always in this condition,
  Sitting home alone with no one there,
With just enough money to eat,
  And afford his monthly rent and heat.

The penthouse and servants had all left,
  His furniture and cars are repossessed,
The youthful eye candy at his side,
  Took his jewelry, furs, and dignity too.

In his life, he lied and cheated,
  To make it to the very top,
His ego was huge and unsurpassed,
  Until he made one big mistake.

The law closed in, and he spewed some hate,
  But no one listened it was too late.
They cheered his sentence, and years to go,
  In cuffs and chains, he went away.

The decades flew by as the sun rose and set,
  Spewing a shadow on a concrete cell floor,
The lawyers stopped coming, or writing him too,
  He sat alone in prison with nothing to do.

Old and bent with no hair to comb,
  The massive steel gates yawned wide open,
As he walked out alone with a bus pass
  To someplace, he wasn't sure where.

The breeze felt good as it swiped by his face,
  He stood by the wall on the other side now.
His name is forgotten; he had a great fall,
  No one came to greet him or welcome him home.

Except for the newspapers
  On page sixty-four,
Which mention he's out,
  And put on the floor
For his dog to lie down.

Brooklyn

The City of Brooklyn is dead; replaced by becoming a borough and joining four other state counties to make the City of New York. Yet buried deep in its exoskeleton is pride of self, a pushy pugilistic demeanor with a dialect unique in the nation and instantly recognizable as an almost distinct language.

With disdain, Manhattan looks down on it, but the reverse is also true. Probably the only borough to think of itself still as an independent part of the whole, superior if you will. Button busting, hardworking, and proud of its brashness; it's citizen's dash to work to all the other boroughs while still thinking they are coming home at night to a more equal of equals' piece of New York City.

The different ethnic and religious areas of Brooklyn are merging at the fringes. Cross-pollinating cultures, foods both zesty Indian or salty kosher amongst others, and foreign national bloodlines coagulating together causing a scab to grow, irritating to some, yet settling in as the new normal; a real American melting pot of colors.

Cigar smoking cabbies with two-day-old gray stubble on their faces and faded newsboy caps covering their balding heads yelling out their open windows are a thing of the past. Today close-cropped hair from foreign-born drivers who barely speak English taxi you around the place like an amusement park ride and deliver you to your destination well shaken, not stirred.

The old farmland of Brooklyn with its cows, pigs, and horses is supplanted by vermin and insects as large as birds, or bigger. The animals in the Brooklyn Zoo are replaced by the ones who roam at night in the crevices of civilization hunting their prey; sometimes on the foul smelling, litter soaked below ground subway stations of the borough with ruthless ease.

The salt air is wafting in from the Atlantic Ocean, waves lapping on the cigarette strewn sand of Coney Island's beaches, and the lovers reclining on blankets under an umbrella embracing while profusely sweating from the hot beating sun.

Exhaust fans of the food vendors on Surf Avenue entice your olfactory glands, and many a mouth begins to salivate until the spittle overflows forcing you to buy something to eat.

The City of Brooklyn is gone, not forgotten, missed, but still proud to be from, and lives on in the memories of its citizens never to be replaced. And, I can't go back.

Congress

When they say they want to help people
  By taking away their health care,
I don't understand how this helps them
  Be healthier and live longer.

When they say they want to kill Medicare,
  Although we pay for it from our income,
Many proclaim it an entitlement, a handout,
  So they can give the money to the rich
And corporations for unneeded tax cuts.
  What am I to think of these people?

When they say they want to reduce Medicaid
  So poor people can't see a doctor;
Or the elderly can't be placed in a nursing home,
  At the end of their life, then what happens to them?

They are Amalekites! Every single one of them,
  Seeking to enrich their wealthy donors at the expense
Or the death of those who elected them to serve the
public good,
  They all deserve the harshest biblical punishment.

Feelings

God, I feel the weight of the world on my shoulders.
I hear the beaten, burned and abused young children
crying.
I read of the brave soldiers killed and mutilated in the
line of duty,
While watching their mothers and wives fill a river with
tears.

The news is full of families hungry and homeless,
Their houses foreclosed, and their savings depleted,
Workers downsized, and unemployment payments
ending,
With bankers and Wall Street still driving their
Bentleys.

What are these people to do with their lives?
For all those unfortunates, I really do care,
I would stand on a mountain and issue this dare,
Take pity, and help, for those that you see,
For someday, somewhere, that person might be me.

The Political Ocean

It was dawn when the ship threw off their long ropes
   The mast is quite rigid, and the sails unfurled
The crew scurried round to handle all their posts
   The captain steadily steered his ship's maiden
voyage.
With calm winter waters, the ship sailed out from the
port
   The investors are waving and cheering back on the
dock
As their ship headed out to a future unknown,
   With hope in their hearts, and adventure ahead.
The year was '08, and the sea started to churn
   With waves growing higher the bow did not yield
The Black Lady Dee had set a true course, and
   Battled on showing no fear or remorse
The waves were as high as the highest full mast
   The crew hung on ropes while the ship plowed
through seas
Slipping between waves, and pitching and rolling
   Ever mindful of the sailors, the captain did steer
While the sea battered hard and tried to take over
   The ship kept its course and did reach its port
The journey is over as the ship returned safely
   It's belly full of cargo the investors had sought.
Prosperity for all and no one was lost
   The ocean tried hard, but it could not stop
The Black Lady Dee on its first term at sea.

Unjust and Deaf

There are hungry children in America,
And people dying due to lack of care.
Where are the politicians trying to help?
Paying for walls and bombs,
And no food or Medicare?
This is an outrage; I cannot say it any stronger.
We send billions to other lands,
But none to our folks in need.
Every person must be fed and covered
Before we do another deed.
It is only money, and there are many,
Who tried for success…and failed.
Where are the religious who sprout
To reach out and help the fallen?
Take pity on our own,
Help those who ask for help,
Vote out the ones, who are deaf to this,
And elect people who have a heart.

The Virgin Annabelle

Hang'em high
 Hang'em long
  These are the words
  To a deadly song

      Looking out through the iron bars of the jail's rear window these words keep tumbling around in his head. The only thing he can focus on at the moment is the outstretched branch of the old oak tree calling to him. The leaves have fallen off; the sky is overcast, and the dark rough-hewn brown bark on the tree limb is worn out in a small circular pattern from where previous ropes were hung.

      Time is fleeting, and he knows it.

      With the virile personality of a cactus and the poison kiss of a rattlesnake, he turns to greet the young Virgin Annabelle who is bringing him his lunch today. Her father is the sheriff, and her mom cooked what will be the last meal for him.

      Standing in front of the cell wearing a small floral patterned ruffled dress, her Sunday best, she calls out to him in a lyrical voice his food is here. Anxious to see a true killer the Virgin Annabelle begged her father to be allowed to bring his food to the jail today for one last time before the execution. In what seems like forever he slowly turns to view the innocent face with lips like cherries, eyes penetratingly gray, and thick brown locks framing her face like a scarf beckoning to him. To her surprise, this killer is only a few years older than she is. Peeking out from under his hat she clearly sees curly unkempt hair like that of a wet dog which just shook himself dry, and a lean body taut and muscular. The eyes of Satan meet hers, and they both are smitten. Eve is back in the Garden of Eden staring at the forbidden fruit, ever so wanting to touch it, to devour it…completely.

Like fire belching from cannons shooting repeatedly during a hectic battle their hormones rage to be let free like a swarm of bees pollinating their flowers. The thick black iron bars separate them for the moment, but not for long. Hidden under the napkin on his tray is a thin wire to pick a lock and escape. Taking the plate he thanks her, and can feel the instrument to his salvation under the spoon.

With a twinkle in her eyes, she bids him a fond adieu and blows him a kiss as she walks out leaving him behind. In haste, he bends the wire and starts to jiggle the lock trying to turn the cylinders. Success, the door opens, and he hesitates but for a moment. Listening with care by the door he does not hear a sound from inside the outer office. With luck, he can make his daring escape.

Running out of his cell, and opening the door to the sheriff's office he views the pretty young Virgin Annabelle standing there alone waiting for him. He is only fifteen feet to Heaven and freedom.

A shot rings out, and his heart is shattered in more ways than one. Annabelle places the pistol on a desk and walks over to him lying on the floor to make sure he is dead. The man he killed at a local saloon was her fiancé, and the Virgin Annabelle, though still a virgin, may not be so virtuous.

Sisters at the Cemetery

Wandering between canyons of gravestones on a mild
November day,
calling out the names of the dead they knew when alive,
I saw them from a distance; separated by aisles of
massive memories
As they walked toward me waving hello amongst the
deceased.

We met at the footstone of their grandparents; they
begin to tell me
about their family's history and offer to donate back the
empty plots
they will never use. As they look down at the name of a
buried child one of them starts to cry.

A ten-year-old boy was run over by a truck and killed
one hundred years ago. There is a huge monument
erected in his
memory. The boy's father bought this land and made it
into a cemetery for his congregation.
The top of the stone monument is missing. Over ten
feet up
there is a flat base with nothing on top.

I explain to them I was told he was killed before
he was a bar mitzvah, so there is no top
on his monument. The young boy is still
considered a child.

The eyes of one sister fill with tears
as a stranger now mourns for a lost childhood,
a lost future, the wasted potential for good which
cannot

be replaced. The other sister stands silently, head
bowed.

I can feel the empathy, the emotions she sheds for
this child she never knew; dead decades before his
parents.
This woman reassures me goodness and kindness
still exists in the chaos of today's world.

It is now time to leave and go back to the office
with both of them to conduct business.

The End

www.ingramcontent.com/pod-product-compliance
Lightning Source LLC
Chambersburg PA
CBHW061755020426
42331CB00024B/1915